Poetry for Young People

Walt Whitman

Edited by Jonathan Levin
Illustrations by Jim Burke

STERLING

New York / London
www.sterlingpublishing.com/kids

For Sam, Emilia, Dustin, and Ellie
—Jonathan

This book is dedicated to Mom and Dad. Thank you for your endless support and inspiration. I love you.
—Jim

I'd like to tip my hat and give thanks to the following models and supporters: Ken Anderson, Jim Burke, Kaitlin Burke, Sean Burke, Cathy Campbell, Nick Covatis, Bob Dacey, Roger DeMuth, Russ Foster, Ron Gagnon, Joe Glisson, Dale Gregory, Dennis Hall, Muriel Herbert, Brian Lavigne, David Lavigne, Kevin Lavigne, Ron Levine, Brandon "Bud" LeBlanc, Scott Lubreque, Sean Marky, Buddy McQuade, Bill Miller, Katie Miller, Susan Miller, Katie O'Connor, Royce Potts, Amanda Powers, Danny Powers, Martial Prosper, Omer "Curly" Roy, Frank Scorupski, Phil Simmons, Kaitlyn Telge, John Thompson, Murray Tinkelman, and Wingspur Ranch.   *—Jim*

STERLING and the distinctive Sterling logo are registered trademarks of
Sterling Publishing Co., Inc.

Library of Congress Cataloging-in-Publication Data
Whitman, Walt, 1819–1892
Walt Whitman : poetry for young people / edited by Jonathan Levin :
Illustrated by Jim Burke.
p   cm.
Includes index.
Summary: An illustrated collection of twenty-six poems and excerpts
from longer poems by the renowned nineteenth-century poet.
ISBN 0-8069-9530-0
1. Children's poetry, American. [1. American poetry.]
I. Levin, Jonathan. II. Burke, Jim, ill.
PS3203.L48 1997
811'.3—dc21   97–433

4 6 8 10 9 7 5 3

First paperback edition published 2008
by Sterling Publishing Co., Inc.
387 Park Avenue South, New York, NY 10016
Text © 1997 by Jonathan Levin
Illustrations © 1997 by Jim Burke
Distributed in Canada by Sterling Publishing
^{c}/$_o$ Canadian Manda Group, 165 Dufferin Street
Toronto, Ontario, Canada M6K 3H6
Distributed in the United Kingdom by GMC Distribution Services
Castle Place, 166 High Street, Lewes, East Sussex, England BN7 1XU
Distributed in Australia by Capricorn Link (Australia) Pty. Ltd.
P.O. Box 704, Windsor, NSW 2756, Australia

Printed in China 09/12
All rights reserved

Sterling ISBN-13: 978-0-8069-9530-4 (trade)
ISBN-10: 0-8069-9530-0

Sterling ISBN-13: 978-1-4027-5477-7 (paper)
ISBN-10: 1-4027-5477-9

For information about custom editions, special sales, premium and
corporate purchases, please contact Sterling Special Sales
Department at 800-805-5489 or specialsales@sterlingpublishing.com.

Contents

WALT WHITMAN: I TRAMP A PERPETUAL JOURNEY

When Walt Whitman began publishing his poems in the mid-1800s, he forever changed people's sense of what a poet could be, and what a poem could look and sound like.

For Whitman, poetry was no school-room or parlor exercise. It wasn't an "indoor" activity at all. Instead, poetry had to breathe the open air. It had to start in the earth, just as a tree sets its roots deep in the soil, and then take flight, just as the tree shoots its branches into the sky.

Whitman liked to think of the poet as a kind of tramp: someone who travelled far and wide, meeting new people along the way, constantly seeking out new experiences and new encounters. He also liked to think of himself as the poet of the common man and woman. He admired people who worked hard, especially people who worked with their hands, and he often even made them the subject of his poems. More than anything else, though, he loved the diversity of life: so many different people, so many different kinds of plants and animals, cities and farms, dreams and visions. As a kind of poetic tramp, Whitman set out to encounter all this variety of life and to make it all hang together in his poems. Nobody had ever before tried to put so much into a poem.

Take a quick look at any poem in this book—just look at it, without even reading it. Whitman's lines almost seem to run right off the page. Before Whitman, the true mark of a poem was its regular pattern of meter and rhyme: the poet sought to shape his emotions and ideas into an organized form. Whitman's long lines are not usually structured in this way. In fact, they often seem to flow across the page in what looks like an uncontrollable flood of words. This happens because he is always trying to get so much of the detail of his world into his poems.

Read these poems aloud. Try to catch the sound of Whitman's voice in them. Whitman is said to have recited poetry aloud as he walked along the Long Island sea shore, and you can sometimes almost hear the rhythm of the surf in his poems. You can also sometimes hear the voice of a prophet, as when he cries out, "Unscrew the locks from the doors! Unscrew the doors themselves from the jambs!" Whitman loved the sound of the human voice, in speech and in song, and always imagined himself "singing" aloud in his poems.

Walt Whitman was born at West Hills, Long Island, in New York on May 31, 1819. His father, Walter Whitman, was a carpenter and a house builder, and a staunch supporter of the ideals of the American Revolution. Walt attributed his creativity to the influence of his mother, Louisa Van Velsor Whitman. Walt eventually had seven brothers and sisters, of which he was the second oldest. When Walt was not quite four years old, the Whitmans moved to Brooklyn, New York, where Walt's father continued to build and sell houses. It was a difficult time economically, and Whitman's father suffered many losses selling the houses he built. Walt managed to attend public schools for six years, until the age of eleven, but was forced to go to work as an office boy to earn money for the family after that. This was all the formal education he ever received.

When Walt was six, the Marquis de Lafayette, one of the last surviving heroes from the Revolutionary War, visited Brooklyn for a Fourth of July celebration. According to a story Whitman often told, General Lafayette lifted a number of schoolchildren, including young Walt. In some versions of the story, General Lafayette even embraced the future poet before putting him down. Whitman liked to tell this story, probably because he viewed it as a passing of the torch of freedom from one generation to the next.

At the age of eleven, Whitman went to work at the law offices of James B. Clarke and his son, Edward Clarke. Besides helping Walt with his handwriting and composition, Edward Clarke also signed Walt up with the local lending library, which marks the beginning of Walt's lifelong love of literature. Among his earliest favorites were the *Arabian Nights*, the historical novels and poems of Sir Walter Scott, and the adventure novels of another ground-breaking American writer, James Fenimore Cooper.

After working in law offices and a physician's office, Walt went to work for a newspaper. He began as an apprentice compositor, setting type for various local newspapers. Eventually, beginning in his mid-teens, he also began writing short pieces that appeared in the papers. Like many well-known authors, Whitman began his literary career as a journalist, reporting on a wide variety of topics. He was often asked to review books, operas, and plays during these years, a task that allowed him to indulge in his favorite pastimes: reading and attending the theater, especially opera.

With the continued problems of the real-estate market, Walter Whitman, Sr. moved his family back to Long Island. Walt, still a teenager, stayed behind in Brooklyn to continue working at various newspapers. Eventually, however, he rejoined his family and became a schoolteacher on Long Island. From his late teens into his twenties, Whitman alternated working as a teacher and as a compositor/journalist, depending on the kind of work he could find. Whitman was not your average mid-nineteenth-century schoolteacher. For one thing, he refused to hit his students, which made many local residents suspicious of his "lax" methods as a teacher!

By 1841, Whitman was back again in New York City, working as a compositor and writing stories for the papers. It was at this time that he was assigned to cover the New York City lectures of a visiting New England speaker already famous throughout the country, Ralph Waldo Emerson. Emerson would have a tremendous impact on Whitman's sense of what he could do as a writer. Emerson encouraged his audience to follow their inner promptings in all things. In one of the talks Whitman heard, Emerson called for a new kind of poet, one who would set free the imagination and, by doing so, transform the world.

Whitman worked at many different papers during this period, finding himself forced out of one job because he supported the principle that slavery be prohibited in all newly annexed territories—the very issue that eventually led to the Civil War. Whitman did a brief stint at a New Orleans paper, a period most notable for Whitman's journey to and from New Orleans. He travelled by train to Cumberland, then by horse-drawn stage to Wheeling, West Virginia, where he caught the steamboat that sailed the Ohio and Mississippi Rivers to New Orleans; he returned a little over two months later by steamboat up the Mississippi and across the Great Lakes, where, after taking the train to Niagara and Albany, he caught another steamboat that took him down the Hudson River to Manhattan. Whitman's fascination with American places was energized by these trips.

When his family returned to Brooklyn, Whitman again lived with them, travelling almost daily by ferry to Manhattan. This was the period during which he began to work on his first collection of poems, *Leaves of Grass*, which appeared when Whitman was 36 years old, in 1855. Whitman even assisted in typesetting the volume. The picture that appears in this book on page four, taken from the 1855 collection, depicts Whitman as the working-class man that he took such pride in being, dressed in a work shirt with the collar open, the tilt of his hat indicating his casual and even slightly mischievous air.

Early responses to Whitman's first book were often very critical. The *Boston Intelligencer* printed a scathing review, stating that Whiman "must be some escaped lunatic, raving in pitiable delirium." This was not an uncommon attitude at the time. Whitman was writing an entirely new kind of poetry. Who had ever seen poems about runaway slaves or about the miracles of everyday life, or a poem that began so boldly as "I celebrate myself"? Many readers disapproved of Whitman's subject matter and his style, neither of which seemed to them "refined" or "lofty" enough.

But Whitman also had his supporters. One of them was none other than Ralph Waldo Emerson, who had done so much to inspire Whitman in the first place. Emerson wrote Whitman a letter calling the book "the most extraordinary piece of wit and wisdom that America has yet contributed." "I greet you at the beginning of a great career," Emerson wrote, perhaps recognizing in Whitman the very poet he had called for in his lecture "The Poet."

Whitman was so fond of this letter that he had it reprinted in the second edition of his *Leaves of Grass*. Unfortunately, he never asked Emerson's permission, which upset Emerson, since it had in fact been written in personal correspondence. The two never managed to develop much of a friendship after that, and Emerson eventually even joked that Whitman was "half song-thrush, half alligator."

Whitman's father died on July 11, 1855, just days after *Leaves of Grass* appeared, leaving Walt to provide for his mother and siblings. Whitman would suffer financial difficulties for much of the rest of his life. He borrowed money and worked when he could as a newspaper editor. In 1860, a Boston publisher offered to print a third edition of *Leaves of Grass*. Whitman earned an impressive $1,000 from this edition, but the publishers went bankrupt shortly after publishing the book, and once again Whitman was strapped for money.

Over the years, Whitman published several editions of *Leaves of Grass*, revising old poems and adding new ones to the constantly growing collection. In all, Whitman published nine editions of *Leaves of Grass* in his lifetime.

Soon after Whitman prepared the 1860 edition, his brother George was wounded fighting in the battle of Fredericksburg in the Civil War. Whitman went to Washington, D.C. to be with George, who was recovering in a field hospital from a wound to the cheek. In Washington, Whitman was drawn into the orbit of the war, not as a soldier, but as a volunteer nurse. He worked as a clerk at a government office in the morning and visited the wounded in the Washington hospitals in the afternoon. He assisted these soldiers in any way he could, bringing them small gifts, talking with them, and occasionally writing out letters to family members that the soldiers would dictate to him (much like the letter in "Come Down from the Fields Father, page 31).

The Civil War (1861-1865) proved to be a crucial period in Whitman's life. Long a vocal opponent of slavery, he was also, like Abraham Lincoln, a determined supporter of the Union. Lincoln became another great hero to Whitman. Stories about Lincoln's own admiration of Whitman have also been told, but these probably have more legend in them than truth. Whitman himself claimed that he and Lincoln would regularly "exchange bows, and very cordial ones." In any event, Whitman admired Lincoln's force of character and his effort to bring an end to slavery and preserve the Union. Devastated when the President was assassinated in 1865—Whitman called it the "crowning crime of the Rebellion"—he wrote some of his best poems to mourn the passing of Lincoln (see "O Captain! My Captain!" and "When Lilacs Last in the Dooryard Bloom'd," pages 38 and 40).

After working as an office clerk in Washington, D.C. for several years, Whitman suffered a stroke in 1873. He moved to Camden, New Jersey soon after the stroke, where his mother died within three days of his arrival. Whitman would spend the rest of his days, apart from occasional travel, in Camden, often receiving visitors, with whom he was always happy to pass an afternoon in conversation. He made an extraordinary impression on his visitors, confirming his informal title as "The Good Gray Poet."

Whitman never married and is generally believed never to have had any children. By the time he died in 1892, he was widely regarded as one of the most important and accomplished, and one of the best loved writers America had yet produced.

I HEAR AMERICA SINGING

Whitman printed this as one of several poems that introduce his Leaves of Grass. *Notice the diversity of voices that make up Whitman's image of "America Singing."*

I hear America singing, the varied carols I hear,
Those of mechanics, each one singing his as it should be blithe and strong,
The carpenter singing his as he measures his plank or beam,
The mason singing his as he makes ready for work, or leaves off work,
The boatman singing what belongs to him in his boat, the deckhand singing on the steamboat deck,
The shoemaker singing as he sits on his bench, the hatter singing as he stands,
The wood-cutter's song, the ploughboy's on his way in the morning, or at noon intermission or at sun-
    down,
The delicious singing of the mother, or of the young wife at work, or of the girl sewing or washing,
Each singing what belongs to him or her and to none else,
The day what belongs to the day—at night the party of young fellows, robust, friendly,
Singing with open mouths their strong melodious songs.

blithe—*happy, carefree*   melodious—*musical*

On Land

O the gleesome saunter over fields and hillsides!
The leaves and flowers of the commonest weeds, the moist fresh stillness of the woods,
The exquisite smell of the earth at daybreak, and all through the forenoon.

—from "A Song of Joys"

MIRACLES

With a little imagination, you can always finds miracles in what seems most ordinary and plain. Whitman uses one of his favorite poetic devices here, the catalogue, to demonstrate just how many miracles we encounter every day.

Why, who makes much of a miracle?
As to me I know of nothing else but miracles,
Whether I walk the streets of Manhattan,
Or dart my sight over the roofs of houses toward the sky,
Or wade with naked feet along the beach just in the edge of the water,
Or stand under trees in the woods,
Or talk by day with any one I love, or sleep in the bed at night with any one I love,
Or sit at table at dinner with the rest,
Or look at strangers opposite me riding in the car,
Or watch honey-bees busy around the hive of a summer forenoon,
Or animals feeding in the fields,
Or birds, or the wonderfulness of insects in the air,
Or the wonderfulness of the sundown, or of stars shining so quiet and bright,
Or the exquisite delicate thin curve of the new moon in spring;
These with the rest, one and all, are to me miracles,
The whole referring, yet each distinct and in its place.

To me every hour of the light and dark is a miracle,
Every cubic inch of space is a miracle,
Every square yard of the surface of the earth is spread with the same,
Every foot of the interior swarms with the same.

To me the sea is a continual miracle,
The fishes that swim—the rocks—the motion of the waves—the ships with men in them,
What stranger miracles are there?

SONG OF MYSELF

"Song of Myself" is the first poem of Whitman's first book. It is made up of 52 sections, of which the first, sixth, and ninth are given here. These sections use the image of the grass and hay as symbol for the never-ending processes of life and death.

I celebrate myself, and sing myself,
And what I assume you shall assume,
For every atom belonging to me as good belongs to you.

I loafe and invite my soul,
I lean and loafe at my ease observing a spear of summer grass.

❖   ❖   ❖

A child said *What is the grass?* fetching it to me with full hands;
How could I answer the child? I do not know what it is any more than he.
I guess it must be the flag of my disposition, out of hopeful green stuff woven.

Or I guess it is the handkerchief of the Lord,
A scented gift and remembrancer designedly dropt,
Bearing the owner's name someway in the corners, that we
        may see and remark, and say *Whose?*

Or I guess the grass is itself a child, the produced babe of the vegetation.

Or I guess it is a uniform hieroglyphic,
And it means, Sprouting alike in broad zones and narrow zones,
Growing among black folks as among white,
Kanuck, Tuckahoe, Congressman, Cuff, I give them the same,
        I receive them the same.

And now it seems to me the beautiful uncut hair of graves.

Tenderly will I use you curling grass,
It may be you transpire from the breasts of young men,
It may be if I had known them I would have loved them,
It may be you are from old people, or from offspring taken soon out of their mothers' laps,
And here you are the mothers' laps.

This grass is very dark to be from the white heads of old mothers,
Darker than the colorless beards of old men,
Dark to come from under the faint red roofs of mouths.

O I perceive after all so many uttering tongues,
And I perceive they do not come from the roofs of mouths for nothing.

I wish I could translate the hints about the dead young men and women,
And the hints about old men and mothers, and the offspring taken soon out of their laps.

What do you think has become of the young and old men?
And what do you think has become of the women and children?

They are alive and well somewhere,
The smallest sprout shows there is really no death,
And if ever there was it led forward life, and does not wait at the end to arrest it,
And ceas'd the moment life appear'd.

All goes onward and outward, nothing collapses,
And to die is different from what any one supposed, and luckier.

❖ ❖ ❖

The big doors of the country barn stand open and ready,
The dried grass of the harvest-time loads the slow-drawn wagon,
The clear light plays on the brown gray and green intertinged,
The armfuls are pack'd to the sagging mow.

I am there, I help, I came stretch'd atop of the load,
I felt its soft jolts, one leg reclined on the other,
I jump from the cross-beams and seize the clover and timothy,
And roll head over heels and tangle my hair full of wisps.

hieroglyphic: *ancient Egyptian picture-writing system,*
    difficult to decipher; a "uniform hieroglyphic" would
    refer to the same mystery in all places.
Kanuck—*French Canadian*
Tuckahoe—*Tidewater Virginian (from "tuckahoe," an*
    edible fungus native to Virginia)

Cuff—*African American*
intertinged—*mixed*
transpire: *to come or grow*

SPARKLES FROM THE WHEEL

A crowd of children gathers around a knife-grinder who has set up the tools of his trade on a city streetcorner. The "sparkles from the wheel" are caused by the knife as it is sharpened against the turning grindstone.

Where the city's ceaseless crowd moves on the livelong day,
Withdrawn I join a group of children watching, I pause aside with them.

By the curb toward the edge of the flagging,
A knife-grinder works at his wheel sharpening a great knife,
Bending over he carefully holds it to the stone, by foot and knee,
With measur'd tread he turns rapidly, as he presses with light but firm hand,
Forth issue then in copious golden jets,
Sparkles from the wheel.

The scene and all its belongings, how they seize and affect me,
The sad sharp-chinn'd old man with worn clothes and broad shoulder-band of leather,
Myself effusing and fluid, a phantom curiously floating, now here absorb'd and arrested,
The group, (an unminded point set in a vast surrounding,)
The attentive, quiet children, the loud, proud, restive base of the streets,
The low hoarse purr of the whirling stone, the light-press'd blade,
Diffusing, dropping, sideways-darting, in tiny showers of gold,
Sparkles from the wheel.

flagging—*the pavement*   restive—*restless*
copious—*plentiful*   diffusing—*spreading out*
effusing—*overflowing*

To a Locomotive in Winter

This and the next poem are presented as recitatives, or formal oral presentations, usually made before an audience. Whitman's description captures the force and beauty of the train, almost as if it were a living creature. Indeed, the train almost seems to come to life in the poem.

Thee for my recitative,
Thee in the driving storm even as now, the snow, the winter-day declining,
Thee in thy panoply, thy measur'd dual throbbing and thy beat convulsive,
Thy black cylindric body, golden brass and silvery steel,
Thy ponderous side-bars, parallel and connecting rods, gyrating, shuttling at thy sides,
Thy metrical, now swelling pant and roar, now tapering in the distance,
Thy great protruding head-light fix'd in front,
Thy long, pale, floating vapor-pennants, tinged with delicate purple,
The dense and murky clouds out-belching from thy smoke-stack,
Thy knitted frame, thy springs and valves, the tremulous twinkle of thy wheels,
Thy train of cars behind, obedient, merrily following,
Through gale or calm, now swift, now slack, yet steadily careering;
Type of the modern—emblem of motion and power—pulse of the continent,
For once come serve the Muse and merge in verse, even as here I see thee,
With storm and buffeting gusts of wind and falling snow,
By day thy warning ringing bell to sound its notes,
By night thy silent signal lamps to swing.

Fierce-throated beauty!
Roll through my chant with all thy lawless music, thy swinging lamps at night,
Thy madly-whistled laughter, echoing, rumbling like an earth-quake, rousing all,
Law of thyself complete, thine own track firmly holding,
(No sweetness debonair of tearful harp or glib piano thine,)
Thy trills of shrieks by rocks and hills return'd,
Launch'd o'er the prairies wide, across the lakes,
To the free skies unpent and glad and strong.

panoply—*magnificent attire*
ponderous—*heavy*
gyrating—*turning*
metrical—*rhythmic*

vapor-pennants—*trailing smoke*
careering—*rushing forward*
debonair—*charming*

THE OX-TAMER

Before there were tractors, farmers used oxen to pull their ploughs. These oxen had to be trained. Whitman expresses his admiration for the ox-tamer's abilities, and manages to put in a few words for the great beauty of the oxen themselves.

In a far-away northern county in the placid pastoral region,
Lives my farmer friend, the theme of my recitative, a famous tamer of oxen,
There they bring him the three-year-olds and the four-year-olds to break them,
He will take the wildest steer in the world and break him and tame him,
He will go fearless without any whip where the young bullock chafes up and down the yard,
The bullock's head tosses restless high in the air with raging eyes,
Yet see you! how soon his rage subsides—how soon this tamer tames him;
See you! on the farms hereabout a hundred oxen young and old, and he is the man who has tamed them,
They all know him, all are affectionate to him;
See you! some are such beautiful animals, so lofty looking;
Some are buff-color'd, some mottled, one has a white line running along his back, some are brindled,
Some have wide flaring horns (a good sign)—see you! the bright hides,
See, the two with stars on their foreheads—see, the round bodies and broad backs,
How straight and square they stand on their legs—what fine sagacious eyes!
How they watch their tamer—they wish him near them—how they turn to look after him!
What yearning expression! how uneasy they are when he moves away from them;
Now I marvel what it can be he appears to them, (books, politics, poems, depart—all else departs,)
I confess I envy only his fascination—my silent, illiterate friend,
Whom a hundred oxen love there in his life on farms,
In the northern county far, in the placid pastoral region.

placid—*quiet, tranquil*   mottled—*spotted*
pastoral—*rural*   brindled—*streaked*
break—*to tame or train*   sagacious—*wise*
chafes—*moves restlessly*

A MAN'S BODY AT AUCTION

This poem is part of the longer poem "I Sing the Body Electric," in which Whitman celebrates the human body as an extension of the soul. Here, the speaker describes a slave who is being sold by an auctioneer, a common practice in the South before the Civil War.

A man's body at auction,
(For before the war I often go to the slave-mart and watch the sale,)
I help the auctioneer, the sloven does not half know his business.

Gentlemen look on this wonder,
Whatever the bids of the bidders they cannot be high enough for it,
For it the globe lay preparing quintillions of years without one animal or plant,
For it the revolving cycles truly and steadily roll'd.

In this head the all-baffling brain,
In it and below it the makings of heroes.

Examine these limbs, red, black, or white, they are cunning in tendon and nerve,
They shall be stript that you may see them.

Exquisite senses, life-lit eyes, pluck, volition,
Flakes of breast-muscle, pliant backbone and neck, flesh not flabby, good-sized arms and legs,
And wonders within there yet.

Within there runs blood,
The same old blood! the same red-running blood!
There swells and jets a heart, there all passions, desires, reachings, aspirations,
(Do you think they are not there because they are not express'd in parlors and lecture-rooms?)

This is not only one man, this the father of those who shall be fathers in their turns,
In him the start of populous states and rich republics,
Of him countless immortal lives with countless embodiments and enjoyments.

How do you know who shall come from the offspring of his offspring through the centuries?
(Who might you find you have come from yourself, if you could trace back through the centuries?)

sloven—*an uncultivated person*   volition—*will*
pluck—*courage*

I Think I Could Turn and Live with Animals

Whitman expresses not just his deep love of animals, but also his strong feeling of affinity with them. This poem comes from "Song of Myself."

I think I could turn and live with animals, they are so placid and self-
    contain'd,
I stand and look at them long and long.

They do not sweat and whine about their condition,
They do not lie awake in the dark and weep for their sins,
They do not make me sick discussing their duty to God,
Not one is dissatisfied, not one is demented with the mania of owning things,
Not one kneels to another, nor to his kind that lived thousands of years ago,
Not one is respectable or unhappy over the whole earth.

So they show their relations to me and I accept them,
They bring me tokens of myself, they evince them plainly in their possession.

I wonder where they get those tokens,
Did I pass that way huge times ago and negligently drop them?

Myself moving forward then and now and forever,
Gathering and showing more always and with velocity,
Infinite and omnigenous, and the like of these among them,
Not too exclusive toward the reachers of my remembrancers,
Picking out here one that I love, and now go with him on brotherly terms.

A gigantic beauty of a stallion, fresh and responsive to my caresses,
Head high in the forehead, wide between the ears,
Limbs glossy and supple, tail dusting the ground,
Eyes full of sparkling wickedness, ears finely cut, flexibly moving.

His nostrils dilate as my heels embrace him,
His well-built limbs tremble with pleasure as we race around and return.

I but use you a minute, then I resign you, stallion,
Why do I need your paces when I myself out-gallop them?
Even as I stand or sit passing faster than you.

tokens—*signs, small parts*   omnigenous—*belonging to all types and species*

At Sea

The untold want by life and land ne'er granted,
Now voyager sail thou forth to seek and find.
—"The Untold Want"

ABOARD AT A SHIP'S HELM

Whitman compares the dangerous course of a ship's voyage with the path taken by the immortal soul. The sea is full of hidden dangers for the ship, but a ringing bell at least provides warning. What of the human soul's voyaging?

Aboard at a ship's helm,
A young steersman steering with care.

Through fog on a sea-coast dolefully ringing,
An ocean-bell—O a warning bell, rock'd by the waves.

O you give good notice indeed, you bell by the sea-reefs ringing,
Ringing, ringing, to warn the ship from its wreck-place.

For as on the alert O steersman, you mind the loud admonition,
The bows turn, the freighted ship tacking speeds away under her gray sails,
The beautiful and noble ship with all her precious wealth speeds away gayly and safe.

But O the ship, the immortal ship! O ship aboard the ship!
Ship of the body, ship of the soul, voyaging, voyaging, voyaging.

helm—*ship's steering mechanism*
dolefully—*cheerlessly, sadly*
admonition—*warning*
freighted—*full of freight*

24

THE WORLD BELOW THE BRINE

In describing the world beneath the surface of the sea, Whitman again uses the catalogue, here to emphasize the great variety of life found deep in the sea. In the last two lines of this poem, he speculates about how our human life might appear to beings inhabiting "other spheres" of which we are unaware.

The world below the brine,
Forests at the bottom of the sea, the branches and leaves,
Sea-lettuce, vast lichens, strange flowers and seeds, the thick tangle, openings, and pink turf,
Different colors, pale gray and green, purple, white, and gold, the play of light through the water,
Dumb swimmers there among the rocks, coral, gluten, grass, rushes, and the aliment of the swimmers,
Sluggish existences grazing there suspended, or slowly crawling close to the bottom,
The sperm-whale at the surface blowing air and spray, or disporting with his flukes,
The leaden-eyed shark, the walrus, the turtle, the hairy sea-leopard, and the sting-ray,
Passions there, wars, pursuits, tribes, sight in those ocean-depths, breathing that thick-breathing air, as so
      many do,
The change thence to the sight here, and to the subtle air breathed by beings like us who walk this sphere,
The change onward from ours to that of beings who walk other spheres.

brine—*sea-water*
gluten—*glutenous or gummy substances*
aliment—*food*
disporting—*playing*
flukes—*a whale's tail*

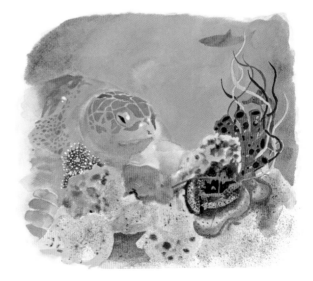

ON THE BEACH AT NIGHT

As clouds darken the starry sky, the speaker consoles a child with a lesson in things eternal. The sea and sky often bring out the mystic in Whitman.

On the beach at night,
Stands a child with her father,
Watching the east, the autumn sky.

Up through the darkness,
While ravening clouds, the burial clouds, in black masses spreading,
Lower sullen and fast athwart and down the sky,
Amid a transparent clear belt of ether yet left in the east,
Ascends large and calm the lord-star Jupiter,
And nigh at hand, only a very little above,
Swim the delicate sisters the Pleiades.

From the beach the child holding the hand of her father,
Those burial-clouds that lower victorious soon to devour all,
Watching, silently weeps.

Weep not, child,
Weep not, my darling,
With these kisses let me remove your tears,
The ravening clouds shall not long be victorious,
They shall not long possess the sky, they devour the stars only in apparition,
Jupiter shall emerge, be patient, watch again another night, the Pleiades shall emerge,
They are immortal, all those stars both silvery and golden shall shine out again,
The great stars and the little ones shall shine out again, they endure,
The vast immortal suns and the long-enduring pensive moons shall again shine.

Then dearest child mournest thou only for Jupiter?
Considerest thou alone the burial of the stars?

Something there is,
(With my lips soothing thee, adding I whisper,
I give thee the first suggestion, the problem and indirection,)
Something there is more immortal even than the stars,
(Many the burials, many the days and nights, passing away,)
Something that shall endure longer even than lustrous Jupiter,
Longer than sun or any revolving satellite,
Or the radiant sisters the Pleiades.

---

ravening—*devouring*
athwart—*across*
Pleiades—*a constella-tion named for the seven daughters of Atlas*
pensive—*thoughtful, dreamy*

Did You Read in the Seabooks...

Taken from "Song of Myself," this poem tells the story of the thrilling revolutionary-war sea battle between the American Serapis *and the British* BonHomme Richard.

Did you read in the seabooks of the oldfashioned frigate-fight?
Did you learn who won by the light of the moon and stars?

Our foe was no skulk in his ship, I tell you,
His was the English pluck, and there is no tougher or truer, and never was, and never will be;
Along the lowered eve he came, horribly raking us.

We closed with him....the yards entangled....the cannon touched,
My captain lashed fast with his own hands.

We had received some eighteen-pound shots under the water,
On our lower-gun-deck two large pieces had burst at the first fire, killing all around and blowing up overhead.

Ten o'clock at night, and the full moon shining and the leaks on the gain, and five feet of water reported,
The master-at-arms loosing the prisoners confined in the after-hold to give them a chance for themselves.

The transit to and from the magazine was now stopped by the sentinels,
They saw so many strange faces they did not know whom to trust.

Our frigate was afire....the other asked if we demanded quarters? if our colors were struck and the fighting done?

I laughed content when I heard the voice of my little captain,
We have not struck, he composedly cried, We have just begun our part of the fighting.

Only three guns were in use,
One was directed by the captain himself against the enemy's mainmast,
Two well-served with grape and canister silenced his musketry and cleared his decks.

The tops alone seconded the fire of this little battery, especially the maintop,
They all held out bravely during the whole of the action.

Not a moment's cease,
The leaks gained fast on the pumps....the fire eat toward the powder-magazine,
One of the pumps was shot away....it was generally thought we were sinking.

Serene stood the little captain,
He was not hurried....his voice was neither high nor low,
His eyes gave more light to us than our battle-lanterns.

Toward twelve at night, there in the beams of the moon they surrendered to us.

---

skulk—*coward*
yards—*poles that support the sails*
magazine—*munitions storehouse*
quarter—*merciful treatment in surrender*
struck—*lowered in surrender*
grape and canister—*cannonballs*

At War

I have nourish'd the wounded and sooth'd many a dying soldier,
And at intervals waiting or in the midst of camp,
Composed these songs.

—from "Not Youth Pertains to Me"

COME UP FROM THE FIELDS FATHER

This poem describes the war's devastation from the point of view of a family on a farm in Ohio. By the end of the poem, the focus is almost exclusively on the boy's mother, who must now come to terms with her grief.

Come up from the fields father, here's a letter from our Pete,
And come to the front door mother, here's a letter from thy dear son.

Lo, 'tis autumn,
Lo, where the trees, deeper green, yellower and redder,
Cool and sweeten Ohio's villages with leaves fluttering in the moderate wind,
Where apples ripe in the orchards hang and grapes on the trellis'd vines,
(Smell you the smell of the grapes on the vines?
Smell you the buckwheat where the bees were lately buzzing?)

Above all, lo, the sky so calm, so transparent after the rain, and with wondrous clouds,
Below too, all calm, all vital and beautiful, and the farm prospers well.

Down in the fields all prospers well,
But now from the fields come father, come at the daughter's call,
And come to the entry mother, to the front door come right away.

Fast as she can she hurries, something ominous, her steps trembling,
She does not tarry to smooth her hair nor adjust her cap.

Open the envelope quickly,
O this is not our son's writing, yet his name is sign'd,
O a strange hand writes for our dear son, O stricken mother's soul!
All swims before her eyes, flashes with black, she catches the main words only,
Sentences broken, *gunshot wound in the breast, cavalry skirmish, taken to hospital,*
At present low, but will soon be better.

Ah now the single figure to me,
Amid all teeming and wealthy Ohio with all its cities and farms,
Sickly white in the face and dull in the head, very faint,
By the jamb of a door leans.

Grieve not so, dear mother, (the just-grown daughter speaks through her sobs,
The little sisters huddle around speechless and dismay'd,)
See, dearest mother, the letter says Pete will soon be better.

Alas poor boy, he will never be better, (nor may-be needs to be better, that brave and simple soul,)
While they stand at home at the door he is dead already,
The only son is dead.

But the mother needs to be better,
She with thin form presently drest in black,
By day her meals untouch'd, then at night fitfully sleeping, often waking,
In the midnight waking, weeping, longing with one deep longing,
O that she might withdraw unnoticed, silent from life escape and withdraw,
To follow, to seek, to be with her dear dead son.

ominous—*vaguely frightening*

THE RUNAWAY SLAVE

The speaker here assists a runaway slave, defying federal laws that would have required him to turn the fugitive slave over to the authorities. This poem, taken from "Song of Myself," shows the kind, humanitarian spirit that escaped slaves sometimes encountered in the North.

The runaway slave came to my house and stopt outside,
I heard his motions crackling the twigs of the woodpile,
Through the swung half-door of the kitchen I saw him limpsy and weak,
And went where he sat on a log and led him in and assured him,
And brought water and fill'd a tub for his sweated body and bruis'd feet,
And gave him a room that enter'd from my own, and gave him some coarse clean clothes,
And remember perfectly well his revolving eyes and his awkwardness,
And remember putting plasters on the galls of his neck and ankles;
He staid with me a week before he was recuperated and pass'd north,
I had him sit next me at table, my fire-lock lean'd in the corner.

limpsy—*limp from weakness*   galls—*skin sores*
plasters—*medicated dressing for a wound*   fire-lock—*rifle*

THE ARTILLERYMAN'S VISION

Whitman wrote many poems about the Civil War, which he collected in a section of Leaves of Grass *called "Drum-Taps."*
The speaker in this poem has returned home, but continues to be haunted by powerful memories of the war.

While my wife at my side lies slumbering, and the wars are over long,
And my head on the pillow rests at home, and the vacant midnight passes,
And through the stillness, through the dark, I hear, just hear, the breath of my infant,
There in the room as I wake from sleep this vision presses upon me;
The engagement opens there and then in fantasy unreal,
The skirmishers begin, they crawl cautiously ahead, I hear the irregular snap! snap!
I hear the sounds of the different missiles, the short *t-h-t! t-h-t!* of the rifle-balls,
I see the shells exploding leaving small white clouds, I hear the great shells shrieking as they pass,
The grape like the hum and whirr of wind through the trees, (tumultuous now the contest rages,)
All the scenes at the batteries rise in detail before me again,
The crashing and smoking, the pride of the men in their pieces,
The chief-gunner ranges and sights his piece and selects a fuse of the right time,
After firing I see him lean aside and look eagerly off to note the effect;
Elsewhere I hear the cry of a regiment charging, (the young colonel leads himself this time with brandish'd
    sword,)
I see the gaps cut by the enemy's volleys, (quickly fill'd up, no delay,)
I breathe the suffocating smoke, then the flat clouds hover low concealing all;
Now a strange lull for a few seconds, not a shot fired on either side,
Then resumed the chaos louder than ever, with eager calls and orders of officers,
While from some distant part of the field the wind wafts to my ears a shout of applause, (some special suc-
    cess,)
And ever the sound of the cannon far or near, (rousing even in dreams a devilish exultation and all the old
    mad joy in the depths of my soul,)
And ever the hastening of infantry shifting positions, batteries, cavalry, moving hither and thither,
(The falling, dying, I heed not, the wounded dripping and red I heed not, some to the rear are hobbling,)
Grime, heat, rush, aide-de-camps galloping by or on a full run,
With the patter of small arms, the warning *s-s-t* of the rifles, (these in my vision I hear or see,)
And bombs bursting in air, and at night the vari-color'd rockets.

grape—*artillery*   fuse—*combustible cord used to light cannons*
batteries—*artillery unit*   volleys—*simultaneous gunfire*
pieces—*weapons*   aide-de-camps—*assistants to commanders*

O Captain! My Captain!

Although he is never mentioned by name, Abraham Lincoln is the subject of this and the following poem. Lincoln was assassinated on April 14, 1865, less than a week after the war had ended. This poem is one of Whitman's few poems written in meter and rhyme.

O Captain! my Captain! our fearful trip is done,
The ship has weather'd every rack, the prize we sought is won,
The port is near, the bells I hear, the people all exulting,
While follow eyes the steady keel, the vessel grim and daring;
　　　　But O heart! heart! heart!
　　　　 O the bleeding drops of red,
　　　　　Where on the deck my Captain lies,
　　　　　 Fallen cold and dead.

O Captain! my Captain! rise up and hear the bells;
Rise up—for you the flag is flung—for you the bugle trills,
For you bouquets and ribbon'd wreaths—for you the shores a-crowding,
For you they call, the swaying mass, their eager faces turning;
　　　　Here Captain! dear father!
　　　　 This arm beneath your head!
　　　　　It is some dream that on the deck,
　　　　　 You've fallen cold and dead.

My Captain does not answer, his lips are pale and still,
My father does not feel my arm, he has no pulse nor will,
The ship is anchor'd safe and sound, its voyage closed and done,
From fearful trip the victor ship comes in with object won;
　　　　Exult O shores, and ring O bells!
　　　　 But I with mournful tread,
　　　　　Walk the deck my Captain lies,
　　　　　 Fallen cold and dead.

WHEN LILACS LAST IN THE DOORYARD BLOOM'D

After his death, Lincoln's body was taken on a long procession from Washington, D.C. through several major American cities. The procession ended in Springfield, Illinois, where he was buried. It was spring, and lilacs, a common dooryard flower, were in bloom. The lilacs became Whitman's symbol for the mourning nation's enduring affection for Lincoln. These passages are drawn from a longer poem on Lincoln's death.

When lilacs last in the dooryard bloom'd,
And the great star early droop'd in the western sky in the night,
I mourn'd, and yet shall mourn with ever-returning spring.

Ever-returning spring, trinity sure to me you bring,
Lilac blooming perennial and drooping star in the west,
And thought of him I love.

❖ ❖ ❖

Coffin that passes through lanes and streets,
Through day and night with the great cloud darkening the land,
With the pomp of the inloop'd flags with the cities draped in black,
With the show of the States themselves as of crape-veil'd women standing,
With processions long and winding and the flambeaus of the night,
With the countless torches lit, with the silent sea of faces and the unbared heads,
With the waiting depot, the arriving coffin, and the sombre faces,
With dirges through the night, with the thousand voices rising strong and solemn,
With all the mournful voices of the dirges pour'd around the coffin,
The dim-lit churches and the shuddering organs—where amid these you journey,
With the tolling tolling bells' perpetual clang,
Here, coffin that slowly passes,
I give you my sprig of lilac.

dooryard—*area around the doorway to a house*   flambeaus—*flaming torches*
great star—*Venus, a symbol here for Lincoln*   sombre—*serious, gloomy*
inloop'd—*looped, or fastened, together*   dirges—*funeral songs*

Sky and Cosmos

After the dazzle of day is gone,
Only the dark, dark night shows to my eyes the stars;
After the clangor of organ majestic, or chorus, or perfect band,
Silent, athwart my soul, moves the symphony true.

— "After the Dazzle of Day"

A NOISELESS PATIENT SPIDER

Whitman develops an analogy between the spider, with its capacity to launch its web into the unknown, and the human soul. What kind of filaments does the human soul send forth?

A noiseless patient spider,
I mark'd where on a little promontory it stood isolated,
Mark'd how to explore the vacant vast surrounding,
It launch'd forth filament, filament, filament, out of itself,
Ever unreeling them, ever tirelessly speeding them.

And you O my soul where you stand,
Surrounded, detached, in measureless oceans of space,
Ceaselessly musing, venturing, throwing, seeking the spheres to connect them,
Till the bridge you will need be form'd, till the ductile anchor hold,
Till the gossamer thread you fling catch somewhere, O my soul.

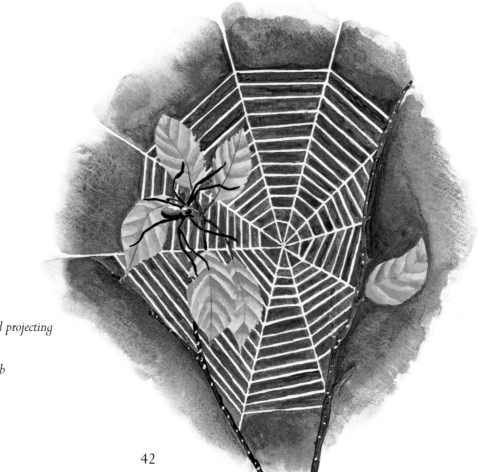

promontory—*a high point of land projecting over water or lower land*
filament—*a thread; the spider's web*
ductile—*easily shaped*
gossamer—*light and delicate*

THE DALLIANCE OF THE EAGLES

*Whitman describes an encounter between two eagles, joined together,
high up in the sky, in a thrilling, playful, loving dance.*

Skirting the river road, (my forenoon walk, my rest,)
Skyward in air a sudden muffled sound, the dalliance of the eagles,
The rushing amorous contact high in space together,
The clinching interlocking claws, a living, fierce, gyrating wheel,
Four beating wings, two beaks, a swirling mass tight grappling,
In tumbling turning clustering loops, straight downward falling,
Till o'er the river pois'd, the twain yet one, a moment's lull,
A motionless still balance in the air, then parting, talons loosing,
Upward again on slow-firm pinions slanting, their separate diverse flight,
She hers, he his, pursuing.

dalliance—*playful, sometimes romantic, activity*
amorous—*loving*
gyrating—*revolving, turning*

talons—*claws*
pinions—*wings*

WHEN I HEARD THE LEARN'D ASTRONOMER

Whitman juxtaposes the scientific lectures he attends on the subject of astronomy with his first-hand experience of the star-filled sky. He discovers something in the first-hand experience that the lectures cannot convey.

When I heard the learn'd astronomer,

When the proofs, the figures, were ranged in columns before me,

When I was shown the charts and diagrams, to add, divide, and measure them,

When I sitting heard the astronomer where he lectured with much applause in the lecture-room,

How soon unaccountable I became tired and sick,

Till rising and gliding out I wander'd off by myself,

In the mystical moist night-air, and from time to time,

Look'd up in perfect silence at the stars.

I TRAMP A PERPETUAL JOURNEY

This poem, taken from "Song of Myself," explores one of Whitman's favorite themes, the romance of travelling the open road. One of Whitman's key ideas here is that you must travel the road "for yourself."

I tramp a perpetual journey, (come listen all!)
My signs are a rain-proof coat, good shoes, and a staff cut from the woods,
No friend of mine takes his ease in my chair,
I have no chair, no church, no philosophy,
I lead no man to a dinner-table, library, exchange,
But each man and each woman of you I lead upon a knoll,
My left hand hooking you round the waist,
My right hand pointing to landscapes of continents and the public road.

Not I, not any one else can travel that road for you,
You must travel it for yourself.

It is not far, it is within reach,
Perhaps you have been on it since you were born and did not know,
Perhaps it is everywhere on water and on land.

Shoulder your duds dear son, and I will mine, and let us hasten forth,
Wonderful cities and free nations we shall fetch as we go.

If you tire, give me both burdens, and rest the chuff of your hand on my hip,
And in due time you shall repay the same service to me,
For after we start we never lie by again.

This day before dawn I ascended a hill and look'd at the crowded heaven,
And I said to my spirit *When we become the enfolders of those orbs, and the pleasure and knowledge of every thing in them, shall we be fill'd and satisfied then?*
And my spirit said, *No, we but level that lift to pass and continue beyond.*

duds—*clothes*   level that lift—*reach that height*
chuff—*probably the palm*

THE SPOTTED HAWK SWOOPS BY

The speaker compares himself to a hawk in this poem that concludes the long sequence "Song of Myself." Whitman takes leave of his reader, but promises to "return" in the form of the many reminders of the themes and images of his poems that the reader (you!) will encounter in the future.

The spotted hawk swoops by and accuses me, he complains of my gab and my loitering.

I too am not a bit tamed, I too am untranslatable,
I sound my barbaric yawp over the roofs of the world.

The last scud of day holds back for me,
It flings my likeness after the rest and true as any on the shadow'd wilds,
It coaxes me to the vapor and the dusk.

I depart as air, I shake my white locks at the runaway sun,
I effuse my flesh in eddies, and drift it in lacy jags.

I bequeath myself to the dirt to grow from the grass I love,
If you want me again look for me under your boot-soles.
You will hardly know who I am or what I mean,
But I shall be good health to you nevertheless,
And filter and fibre your blood.

Failing to fetch me at first keep encouraged,
Missing me one place search another,
I stop somewhere waiting for you.

gab—*pointless talk*   effuse—*to pour out*
yawp—*scream*   eddies—*small whirlpools*
scud—*a slight sudden shower or gust of wind*

Index